BACKPACKER

Hiking and Backpacking
with Kids

PROVEN STRATEGIES FOR FUN FAMILY ADVENTURES

Molly Absolon

FALCONGUIDES

GUILFORD, CONNECTICUT
HELENA, MONTANA
AN IMPRINT OF GLOBE PEQUOT PRESS

FALCONGUIDES ®

Copyright © 2012 by Morris Book Publishing, LLC

Backpacker is a registered trademark of Cruz Bay Publishing, Inc.
FalconGuides is an imprint of Globe Pequot Press.
Falcon, FalconGuides, and Outfit Your Mind are registered trademarks of Morris
Book Publishing, LLC.

Text design: Sheryl P. Kober
Page layout: Justin Marciano
Project editor: Julie Marsh

Library of Congress Cataloging-in-Publication Data

Absolon, Molly.
 Backpacker magazine's hiking and backpacking with kids : proven strategies for
fun family adventures / Molly Absolon.
    p. cm.
 Includes index.
 ISBN 978-0-7627-7295-7
1. Hiking for children. 2. Backpacking. 3. Family recreation. I. Title.
GV199.54.A27 2012
796.51083—dc23

                                                                   2011024257

Printed in China

10 9 8 7 6 5 4 3 2 1

Contents

The author with her daughter, Avery, hiking in Canyonlands National Park when Avery was eighteen months old.

PETER ABSOLON

Introduction

I remember staring up at Mount Baker from a beach in Port Townsend, Washington, eight months into my pregnancy and experiencing this sinking feeling of dread. I thought I was never going to be able to climb a mountain again. As my belly had grown, my world seemed to shrink. I'd been an outdoor professional for all of my adult life, sleeping most nights camped out under the stars. Now suddenly I was having trouble bending over to tie my shoes—to say nothing of the difficulty I had strapping a hip belt around my blossoming middle.

Anyone who has a child can probably empathize with my silly fears. I knew rationally that my life wasn't ending just because we were having a kid, but when it's your first one and your body is doing all these strange, miraculous, but kind of freaky things, you can't help but worry. For me the number one worry was: Would I be able to get back into the wilderness with a baby?

The answer was yes, of course. My life changed dramatically with the arrival of Avery, but within a few weeks we were going for hikes, and at eighteen months, she did her first backpacking trip. There were definitely significant differences in our routines: Our hiking distances shrank and our list of essentials morphed as we were forced to include diapers, wipes, snacks, toys, and endless changes of clothing for those inevitable spills and accidents. But we were still getting out there.

And the best part of hiking and camping with kids? Your whole experience of the outdoors changes. You see things you never noticed before: the cool way ants carry giant loads and rocks shine in water, the amazing athletic ability of squirrels leaping through the trees, and the intricate patterns formed by leaves interlaced overhead. Your entire worldview shifts to that of your child's. Suddenly your legs are 12 inches long and ferns become giant trees, while nooks and crannies in moss-covered rocks are transformed into fairy houses. We once stormed a castle on Harney Peak in South Dakota's Black Hills to free the captive princess. The castle was an old Civilian Conservation Corps–built stone fire lookout on the summit that easily metamorphosed into the lair of an evil witch and captivated our imaginations for a good hour or so of the walk.

The adventures I've shared hiking with my child have generated some of the most memorable and treasured moments we've spent as a family. While tramping through the woods with my daughter, I rediscovered the joy and magic of nature—something I'd kind of lost in my search to pound out long miles, climb challenging peaks, and accomplish various goals. And on top of all that, we were away from the television, away from piles of plastic toys and electronic gadgets, and away from fast food and soda, spending time together.

Kids' curiosity is infectious. You'll soon find yourself on your hands and knees with them looking at things you never noticed before.
SCOTT KANE

When I first started writing this book, I asked my daughter, who is now ten, what she liked best about hiking and backpacking. She mentioned that she loved seeing wild animals and birds, being away from towns and lights, and feeling like an explorer. She said it made her feel proud to have people comment on how impressed they were by her hiking ability and she loved the feeling of being on top of a mountain, relishing that sense of accomplishment she got from achieving a goal.

I'm not sure she would have said these same things when she was younger. Our early outdoor experiences were much more focused and internal, more about play, exploration, and fun than accomplishments. But even as a toddler, she loved to get all cozy in her sleeping bag inside a tent sipping hot chocolate. She loved the intimacy camping brought our family, and from an early age she recognized that the quiet times we spent together outdoors—quiet times when we had no to-do lists, no meetings to get to or deadlines to meet—were special.

What your children, your family, and you get out of camping and backpacking will change with time, but I am convinced that for most of us, just being out in nature brings families together in a way that is difficult to achieve in the bustle of our everyday lives.

Time spent with your children away from the distractions of life back home is priceless. SCOTT KANE

Sure, hiking and backpacking with kids takes a little more work than it took in the days when all you had to worry about was yourself. You definitely have to plan ahead; and spontaneity can be challenging, at least until you get your systems down. But the rewards vastly outweigh the challenges. Your adventures will create memories the entire family will share. You'll have an opportunity to build lasting bonds between you and your children. And you will help your child develop invaluable skills and an appreciation for nature.

ABOUT THIS BOOK

This book brings together all sorts of ideas about hiking and backpacking with kids, and will be useful whether you are just starting out, would like to up the ante, or are looking for help in dealing with a recalcitrant child. I talked to lots of parents about their tips and tricks for enjoying the outdoors with their children, and in the process discovered many things I wish I'd thought of when my daughter was young. That's the beauty of this book. There are no hard and fast rules for a successful hiking or backpacking trip with children, but there are lots of incredibly creative ways to make it easier and more fun. And since a kid's attention span lasts about fifteen minutes, the more ideas you have at your disposal, the better.

In this book you'll find suggestions on gear, clothing, and food. We've covered some basic first-aid tips and risk-management issues specific to children. There's a section on what to look for in a destination and what kinds of trails are best suited for little ones, big kids, and even tweens. But maybe the best information this book contains is the section with tips for entertaining your child on the trail.

Last winter when my daughter was nine, she hiked 23 miles over two passes with significant elevation gain in two days. I'm not including this information to brag or to imply she's something special (okay, she is, but that's just a mother talking); I include it to make a point. For us to successfully complete this hike, we dug deep into our bag of tricks: We told story after story; we made up fairies; we sang songs; we created a scavenger hunt on the go; we did Mad Libs; and we pulled surprise treats—chocolate being the most popular—out of our packs at critical points. We worked to keep her engaged, and in return she was happy and a joy to be with.

Kids can surprise you with their resilience. Long hard days on the trail are doable if you keep them entertained. MOLLY ABSOLON

Some of the most precious family memories come from time spent together outdoors. SCOTT KANE

Our life in town is scheduled to the minute. We go from school to swimming to dance and art. My most lengthy conversations with Avery take place in the car en route to the next destination. But when we hit the backcountry, time slows down. We share our lives and experience things together in a way that seems to elude us most of the time in town. I suspect that these experiences will always be among our most treasured memories, and so I am a bit evangelical about the power of getting outdoors with your kids.

You don't need to go long distances or tackle difficult objectives to enjoy nature with your child. Exploring your city park is a great first outing. Start small and as you gain confidence in your ability, you can go farther and try harder things. Don't be intimidated.

Chapter One
Getting Started

CHOOSING YOUR DESTINATION

Great outdoor destinations are ones that allow children to use their imagination and run free. Some of the best hikes I had with my daughter were on rock outcrops around our home in Wyoming. She could climb over boulders, slither through slot canyons, and slide down the slickrock—all components of a great outdoor adventure for kids. My own favorite childhood memories of being outdoors also center on rock outcrops that were riddled with caves and tunnels for us to play in.

Look for places that include:

» mossy, ferny, drippy nooks that could house fairies, elves, and leprechauns
» water to splash, swim, and play in
» boulders or rock slabs to climb on
» modest peak ascents with lots of scrambling
» snow to slide on and build things with
» beaches with tidal pools to poke around in or shells to collect
» places with birds and wildlife to watch
» mud or sand to construct castles or just glop around in
» rocky shorelines for skipping stones

Rocky outcrops make natural playgrounds. SCOTT KANE

As your children get older, your destination choices will shift to match their changing interests. You may find they want to go fishing or it may be critical for them to bring a friend along during those social years. Teenagers often respond well to challenges, so a third-class peak ascent that involves scrambling and big views may be just the kind of adventure that gets them

Allow time to explore and play during your hike so children can get the most out of their experience.
MOLLY ABSOLON

excited. You can also bring a rope and set up climbs to provide a fun activity. Find a campsite by a good swimming hole or a natural waterslide. Often teens aren't all that different from adults in the kinds of objectives that motivate them down the trail.

How Far Can You Go?

Appropriate distances are hard to pinpoint. What works for one child may not work for another. Plus when you add in variables such as temperature, distractions, and terrain, you quickly realize that a mile-long hike in one location is very different from a mile-long hike in another. That said, it can be helpful to have a few guidelines for selecting hikes if you are unfamiliar with the trails and need to decide what's appropriate for your child. Don't forget to weigh in your child's skill and experience level when using these guidelines. You probably should not take an eight-year-old on a 9-mile hike if it's her first time.

0–1 year old: When your child is riding on your back, you can go as far as you are willing to walk and as long as your child is willing to sit. Some kids fall right to sleep when they get into a backpack and will snooze there for hours; others need to move around occasionally. Regardless, your hiking ability is probably more important than your child's at this stage.

1–2 years old: Toddlers like freedom, so once they are ambulatory, you can expect they will want to walk on their own for at least part of the time. Realistically, kids this age end up walking less than a mile; bring along your baby backpack so you can carry them farther once they get tuckered out.

2–4 years old: As children gain strength and co-ordination, they can tackle longer hikes. Preschoolers are capable of walking 1 to 2 miles on their own with some encouragement and lots of snacks.

4–6 years old: Kids this age will amaze you. If they are having fun and feel as if hiking is playing, they can tackle a significant hike. Look for routes between 2 and 4 miles long.

6–9 years old: Under the right conditions, children this age can easily hike 5 or 6 miles, more if they are strong, motivated, and having a good time.

9–12 years old: Up to 10 miles is probably the limit. But take care not to turn your hike into a death march or you will quickly dampen their enthusiasm for future adventures.

Recognize Risks to Stay Safe

One thing to consider when choosing a kid-friendly destination in the outdoors is the potential danger you may encounter. An icy mountain stream raging next to your campsite creates a pleasant wilderness atmosphere for adults but can be a death trap for a three-year-old. Likewise a campsite located on a precipitous rocky ledge may have great views and low impact, but you probably won't have a moment of peace during your stay if you can never take your eyes off your toddler.

Anyone who has put pads on the corners of their tables, gates around their woodstoves, and barriers at the top of the stairs knows that kids don't really grasp the idea of danger very well. It's the same in the

Scrambling hikes where the consequences of a fall are minimal are great for keeping kids entertained and parents relaxed.
MOLLY ABSOLON

outdoors. You need to think about potential hazards when choosing an appropriate destination for your hike or campsite.

The big potential killers in the wilderness—for all ages—include:

» drowning
» falls
» exposure

People worry about wild animals—bears, mountain lions, and snakes—and it's true if you are in these animals' habitats you'll want to take some special precautions to avoid encounters. But in fact few people have bad experiences with wild animals. The accounts of attacks are sensational, but the numbers are very, very low. So don't avoid hiking in Yellowstone National Park, for example, because you are afraid of grizzly bears. Be smart, follow basic guidelines, keep tabs on your children, and you will be fine.

In Chapter Seven you'll find detailed information about recognizing and managing risks with children in the backcountry. For now I just want to focus on the idea that you may want to consider potential hazards when selecting a destination to explore with your kids. Wandering along a small babbling brook with a youngster is probably going to be a lot less stressful than hiking along an icy torrent.

Destinations where your children are free to explore and play without constant supervision are great for developing a child's sense of independence and curiosity. SCOTT KANE

That said, the wilderness is a great place to begin teaching your children personal responsibility. There's no better way to learn to take care of your gear than to wake up the morning after a storm to find your boots full of water and your clothes soaking wet. The trick is to make sure the choices your children make are age appropriate and have acceptable consequences. You can let them try crossing a stream on a slippery log if a fall just means getting wet; but if the log goes over a boulder-choked section of whitewater, it's not a good place to learn.

You can discover a lot about your destination by talking to people who've been there, reading guidebooks, and checking out maps. Ask about river crossings, exposed sections of trails, and animal hazards before you go. Start with something mellow. Children don't need a lot of drama in the landscape or challenge in the terrain. They find magic in empty boxes and blankets draped across couches, so it doesn't take much to keep them entertained—and the less stressed by potential hazards you are, the more you'll be able to enjoy the experience with your child.

Your risk tolerance will increase as your kids get older and are better able to understand danger; however, they still might not recognize that an injury 10 miles from the car is a bigger deal than one in the city park. Take some time to discuss with your children the way your location affects your decisions.

It doesn't take a lot to keep kids engaged. These children are "meditating marmots"—a game they made up on the trail to keep themselves entertained. JADE PITTEL

Destinations to Avoid

Our worst family hikes took place on hot, dusty trails where the scenery was monotonous—for example, generic lodgepole-pine forests or sagebrush-covered hillsides—and there was nothing to do except trudge along. That kind of hiking is boring for everyone, but adults are better at hiding their feelings than children are. You'll know pretty quickly if your chosen destination fails the "cool" test with your kids. Avoid the temptation to tough it out, unless you really have no choice. A bad experience can mar your next efforts to get your kids hiking.

Factor in time to go slow and check things out. Logging lots of miles is not going to be high on your child's list of priorities. He or she will want time to poke around an anthill or climb up a boulder. Be flexible. If things aren't working out, change what you are doing. Take a rest break. Eat a snack. Play a game. Turn around and go home. It's okay to abort a trip if you—and more importantly your children—aren't having a good time.

WHEN TO GO

Matching your trip to the season will help ensure its success. Kids will not melt if they get cold and wet or overly hot. They do, however, have a tougher time regulating their body temperature, so extreme conditions can be challenging. You are likely to end up having to work harder if you choose to go winter camping or hiking in a rainstorm. That doesn't mean you should not go, just be prepared to handle the conditions for both yourself and your child. We'll go into more detail on clothes and equipment for children later in this book, but for now, bear in mind that weather conditions will affect your trip and your best bet for an enjoyable experience is to shoot for times when the weather is most stable.

When my daughter was three, we went on a camping trip along the Main Salmon River in Idaho. My friends who'd done the trip before assured me that in August it

Inclement weather does not mean you have to stay home. The right equipment will help you stay warm and dry regardless of conditions. MOLLY ABSOLON

would be hot and we should bring a bare minimum of clothing. We ended up encountering a freak week of rain and 50-degree temperatures. The kids were fine; they played happily on the beach, sand sticking to their rain gear. The conditions were hard on me, however. I was anxious about having enough dry clothing to keep Avery warm, so I slept with her polypropylene long underwear at night and wore her wet socks on my shoulders during the day to help dry things out with my body heat. We often had to stop and set up a shelter at lunchtime to get the kids out of the cold and warm them up with hot chocolate before venturing forth again. In the end the trip was great and the kids loved it, but I was a little shell-shocked after expecting 90-degree temperatures. The main lesson for me was: Plan to venture out with your kids during stable months of the year, but prepare for the worst with some extra clothes, lots of snacks, and a backup in case things don't go exactly as planned.

In addition to weather, bugs can have a huge impact on your trip. Kids are sensitive to insect bites and often end up miserable and itchy after exposure. In some places insects are vectors for disease. Mosquitoes can carry West Nile virus while ticks are

Children are oblivious to the weather if they are comfortable.
CHRIS NORTH

particularly nasty and can be carriers of Lyme disease, Rocky Mountain spotted fever, and Colorado tick fever.

A little bit of research can help you determine the best times of year to visit a particular area to avoid peak bug season. Especially when your children are young, it behooves you to pay attention to this information. The Wind River Mountains in Wyoming, for example, are best visited in August and September if you want to avoid the mosquitoes, while the Green Mountains of Vermont have fewer blackflies in late summer. If you do go when the bugs are thick, make sure to have some kind of screened shelter or tent to provide a sanctuary, carry insect repellent and mesh clothing to protect your skin and ward off the bites, and have some kind of anti-itch cream to help provide relief if your kids do get bit.

WHAT AGE IS BEST?

Any age is good for getting outdoors. Babies aren't fragile; it's okay for them to get dirty. Plus if you are nursing, you don't have to carry extra food for them. Toddlers are full of wonder and joy in discovery, so every little bug or leaf is exciting. Elementary school–aged kids can carry their own gear and travel greater distances, while older children can enjoy independence and freedom in the outdoors that they cannot experience at home. The nature of your trips will change as your child grows, but it's never too early to start and there's something special about every age.

Start hiking with your child on flat, short trails and take your time. MOLLY ABSOLON

If you start your children young, they'll grow up understanding and—if you do it right—loving the outdoors. They won't be fazed by pooping in a cathole or sleeping on the ground. They'll learn to push themselves and develop their own strategies for making the trip fun. They'll acquire skills they can use for the rest of their lives and gain a sense of responsibility from having to cope with challenging conditions. It's a great environment for letting children make their own decisions and, perhaps most important, a wonderful place for you to spend time together.

Chapter Two

Gear for Taking Kids Hiking and Backpacking

One of the first shocks of parenthood for me was all the stuff that I had to carry around whenever we left the house: diapers, wipes, changes of clothes, snacks. This list of essentials can make the idea of backpacking or even hiking with children a bit daunting, but have no fear: It is doable. Especially if you keep track of the items that truly are indispensable and get rid of those you never use.

If you have to carry your children for all or part of a hike, it helps to have some way to transport your camping gear. SCOTT KANE

Your equipment needs will change as your child grows, so it's tricky to come up with a definitive list of things to bring. Maslow's Hierarchy of Needs can be a good way to frame your planning. According to this theory, the foundation for all human behavior is ensuring our physiological needs are met. That is, we must be warm, fed, and sheltered in order to function.

CLOTHING

At home we live in temperature-controlled environments. Cold? Turn up the heat. Hot? Time for the air conditioning. In the outdoors your comfort—and more important your child's comfort—is determined largely by adding and subtracting clothing as conditions change. That means clothing is critical to an enjoyable and safe experience.

Staying Warm

We lose heat from our bodies through radiation, conduction, convection, and evaporation. Radiation is a by-product of our metabolic system. We give off the heat produced by living and breathing. Conduction is the movement of heat from a warm object to a cold one, which means if you sit on a cold rock, your 98.6-degree body will lose heat to the rock. Convection is heat loss to the movement of air or water. It's what makes a windy day feel much colder. And finally, moisture on our skin from sweat or rain evaporates or turns into a gas—cooling us in the process. To keep warm in the outdoors, we have to use clothing to regulate our heat loss. On a cold day this means preventing these mechanisms; on a hot one it means maximizing them.

Remember, children don't always communicate their needs very well, especially babies. I will never forget how terrible I felt after a Thanksgiving Day hike with my one-year-old when I discovered her feet were white from cold. She'd whimpered a little during the hike, but not enough to cause me alarm. So I was shocked when I felt her icy little toes. She was fine, but I realized that if temperatures were chilly enough that I felt cool and needed to exercise to stay warm, I needed to be extra careful about a sedentary child on my back. Don't just ask your kid if he is cold (or hot). Feel his skin, especially the extremities. The key is to think about the environmental conditions that both of you are facing and to anticipate your child's needs.

Cold feet warm quickly on a belly—just be ready for the initial shock of those icy toes against your skin. MOLLY ABSOLON

Dress your child in layers that are easy to take on and off as the temperatures vary. Just as with an adult, your best bet is to have a system with the following components:

» base layer—thin polypropylene, wool, or silk long underwear

» mid-layer—midweight insulating layer such as a wool sweater or a pile pullover and pile pants

» insulating layer—in colder conditions a thick insulated parka with a hood is nice

» wind- or waterproof layer—coated-nylon rain gear or Gore-Tex layer for both top and bottom to block out the wind and keep out the rain. In windy climates, if there's no chance of rain, you may want to consider a breathable wind layer (uncoated nylon shell)

Windproof gear is essential in the mountains where temperatures fluctuate wildly. SCOTT KANE

On top of these basics, you'll want to consider mittens, a hat, and extra dry socks. Obviously you don't need all these things for a mile-long hike along the beach in Baja. Use your judgment and plan for worst-case scenarios, but don't worry about a winter storm in a tropical jungle.

Special Considerations

An adult can probably get by with one set of clothes (specifically the base layers) when you go camping, but for children you'll want backups, since kids have a tendency to find mud and water wherever they go. Two sets of clothes is a minimum. More likely you'll

Kids get dirty. Plan ahead so you have plenty of warm, dry clothes for them to change into. MOLLY DORAN

Dress your children in layers so you can add and subtract clothing as the temperatures change. CHRIS NORTH

want three so your child can have one set on, one set drying, and another kept dry in a pack, just in case.

On a day hike just bring one extra top and bottom and maybe a spare sweater. Dry socks are a good idea on any length excursion to help prevent cold feet and cranky kids.

You don't need to go out and buy expensive long underwear or fancy pile jackets. I always found synthetic footie pajamas worked well as a base layer. The only disadvantage is you have to remove the whole outfit to change a diaper, which can be a cold process in the outdoors. But you also avoid gaps in clothing where cold air can seep in, so it's a toss-up as to what is more desirable.

On little babies, socks or thumbless mittens can work well on their hands. The advantage of socks is that you can pull them up high under their jacket and they'll stay on. With toddlers and little kids, stick to mittens rather than gloves. Their hands will stay much warmer. (Big kids may choose mittens for this reason as well.)

Finally, make sure the clothing you have does not constrict blood flow. Avoid tight bands around wrists or ankles that can result in cold hands and feet.

Staying Cool

According to Buck Tilton, the wilderness medicine guru and author of many books on backcountry first aid, children's thermal regulation systems are less developed than adults; consequently they tend to overheat more quickly than we do. So, not only do you need to worry about children getting cold in the outdoors, you also need to watch that they don't get too hot. For staying warm, synthetic fabrics, wool, and silk work best because they hold heat even when wet and often dry faster than cotton. But it's the opposite in hot climates, where you'll want to dress your child in loose-fitting, light-colored cotton garments to help her stay cool. Have kids wear a sun hat and make sure they drink a lot of water. You can also learn from hot-climate cultures and vary your activity levels to avoid the hours of most intense solar radiation. Hike early in the morning or in the late afternoon to minimize your risk of overheating.

Sun hats and light-colored, loose-fitting cotton clothing help keep kids cool in the heat. You can also seek out shade and avoid going out during the hottest parts of the day to minimize exposure. SCOTT KANE

SHOES

For the most part, kids don't need fancy hiking boots. They'll do just fine in sneakers for hiking down the trail. The hard part about footwear is making sure your kids stay warm and dry. You may want to bring rubber boots for tromping around in wet grass, or neoprene water shoes for letting kids play in streams and lakes without worrying about getting their hiking shoes wet. If you anticipate really wet conditions, galoshes are a good investment. In an emergency you can put plastic bags over your child's socks and put the shoes on top. This will help keep feet dry during an unexpected snowstorm.

Neoprene water shoes protect children's feet while they play in water and allow you to keep hiking shoes dry. SCOTT KANE

Dry socks are critical for comfort, so bring lots. For me nothing feels quite so good as getting into soft fresh socks and lightweight shoes after a long day on the trail. If that feels good to me, it undoubtedly feels good to my daughter as well.

Day Pack Essentials

» diapers (Bring two or three more than you anticipate you'll need, just in case you are out longer than planned or your child goes through more than you believed possible.)

» wipes (Useful for kids of all ages. Pack wipes in a ziplock plastic bag or knot an old bread bag, and throw in an extra plastic bag to hold the trash.)

» sun hat or warm hat (climate dependent)

» extra clothing

» rain gear

» snacks (See Chapter Three for suggestions.)

» toilet kit: plastic trowel, wipes or toilet paper, garbage bag, and hand sanitizer (See Sanitation section later in this chapter.)

» water and water purification kit

» small first-aid kit

FOOD

We'll have a whole section on ideas for kid-friendly food in the outdoors, but I mention food here just to make sure you remember to bring enough snacks. A nursing baby is easy: Mom comes with lunch on board. If your child is not nursing or is past that age, you need to have ample food along for the hike.

Nursing mothers always have a snack ready. WILLY WARNER

Snacks serve a variety of functions: They keep your child's energy up, they are a treat for a job well done, and they can be a bribe for action. Most parents have lured their kids up the trail with enticements such as a candy bar at the top of a hill. Snacks are critical to your enjoyment factor out there. We all know what happens when we wait too long to get dinner on the table: The kids break down into tears and get cranky all because we were a little late getting everyone fed. This effect is multiplied in the outdoors, so bring *lots* of food. And make it fun, tasty stuff so your kids will associate the outdoors with yummy food. I asked a young woman who'd grown up backpacking with her father what her most treasured memories of those trips were and she immediately said, "The food." They had gourmet dinners and special desserts, and as a result she remembered those campfire meals years later with special fondness.

SHELTER

For day hikes you don't have to factor in shelter, but if you are going camping it's the final brick in Maslow's foundation of needs. Most families I know crowd into a tent with their children. You can usually add one extra body to a tent's stated capacity if one of the occupants is a toddler. But once kids get to be six or seven, they'll start to use up a full space, so you will need to consider that when allocating sleeping spaces.

When I was a kid, we had a big canvas tent that leaked if you touched the sides—not a good idea with young children. I remember abandoning our camp in the middle of the night on one family camping trip. We just left the tent, got into the car, and drove to a motel to escape the leaks. Today's tents—even relatively inexpensive ones—are made with more effective materials.

As for sleeping arrangements, small children such as babies and toddlers can usually cuddle up with a parent in a sleeping bag, as long as it is not an extremely narrow mummy bag. You can put zippers on a V-shaped piece of fabric to zip into your bag, expanding it so it accommodates two more easily. Functional Design makes an insulated bag extender called the Sweetie Pie that works well for transforming a single-person mummy bag into a family bag.

Or zip two bags together and put your child in between adults for the night. Once your kid is four or five, this sleeping system will start getting pretty tight. An adult and child can still share comfortably, but you may want to invest in another sleeping bag if you plan to get out a lot. Look for either a child-size sleeping bag or a small adult bag. Don't buy a cheap cotton-lined bag from the discount store. You'll want a decent sleeping bag to ensure your child has a good, warm

You can make—or purchase—a V-shaped extender to zip into your bag so it sleeps an adult and child easily. TRACEY BYRNE

night's rest. Talk to a salesperson to determine what bag is best suited for the type of camping you envision.

BABY CARRIERS

There are all sorts of good baby backpacks on the market. Kelty, Sherpa, Macpac, and Deuter are just some of the names I'm familiar with. The popularity of particular models changes year to year, so it's not worth giving out specifics. But there are a few considerations worth noting before you go out and buy yourself a pack.

» **Weight:** Make sure your baby carrier is not so heavy that adding the child means you are carrying more weight than you can handle. You want your backpack to be sturdy and well made, but also not overbuilt to the point it weighs more than your child.

» **Comfort:** Ask around and see what your friends are using. If you can, try theirs out before making the investment in your own. Like any backpack, baby backpacks need to fit you properly to be comfortable. It behooves you to buy yours from a reputable dealer who can help you with the fit. Cheap carriers often do not have adequate suspension systems, leaving you suffering after a few miles on the trail. Make sure the straps are well sewn, reinforced at wear points, and padded. You'll also want to make sure your child's seat is well padded and comfortable.

» **Storage:** It's nice to have some carrying capacity for snacks, layers, and toys, and a few external pockets for items you want handy, like a water bottle. We sometimes strapped a duffle bag under the child's seat in our carrier to add to our load capacity. If you try this, it's best to use that space for soft, lightweight items such as clothes.

» **Durability:** If you plan to hike a lot with your child, it's worth buying a high-quality backpack. There are definitely cheap knockoffs available, but you suffer in the areas of comfort and longevity if you try to shortchange quality.

» **Sun, wind, and rain protection:** Most carriers come with some kind of cover to protect your child from the elements. Make sure these covers attach securely and provide adequate coverage. You may need to modify the cover if you anticipate lots of wind and sideways rain.

A good baby backpack is one that is comfortable for both the carrier and the rider.

PAUL ABSOLON

Look for a baby backpack with a good suspension system and lots of padding. WILLY WARNER

BACKPACKS FOR KIDS

Every parent I talked to in preparation for this book had a slightly different theory about how much a child should carry and when. For me the bottom line seems to be personality driven. If your child likes to be like the grown-ups and is pretty tough, by all means start her carrying her weight as soon as she shows an interest. I waited until my daughter was eight before asking her to carry a pack and then I started light. She carried a layer, her water, and maybe a snack. As she's gotten older, her load has increased, but I'm still inclined to go light just because I want her to enjoy her hiking experience and I know that enjoyment is diminished by heavy loads and aching shoulders. Furthermore, she isn't the one who has decided to go hiking, I am. If I want her to come along with me, I need to make the activity as fun for her as I can. But not all people agree with my viewpoint. All I can say is, it has worked for us.

A general rule of thumb is 5 pounds body weight per 1 pound on the back. So an 80-pound child could presumably carry 16 pounds. If your child is overweight, you'll want to figure that into your calculation. For example, if your kid weighs 100 pounds but is 10 pounds overweight, you'll want to base your calculation on his ideal weight, in this case 90 pounds, to ensure you aren't overloading him.

Small water-hydration packs such as those made by CamelBak are great for kids. They are roomy

Make sure backpacks fit properly regardless of the size of the individual child's load. DOT NEWTON

enough to carry a few essentials and have the added bonus of making it easy for your child to stay hydrated. These packs are unlikely to have enough capacity for overnight trips if your child is going to carry his or her clothes and a sleeping bag.

If you plan to go backpacking on a regular basis, it's worth investing in a properly fitted backpack. Big outdoor equipment stores such as REI carry child-size backpacks and usually have trained staff to help with fitting. Be careful using cheap school backpacks. They may be fine for simple trips with light loads, but if you want your child to carry 15 pounds or more, you're likely to run into trouble. Most school backpacks do not have a hip belt, which means all the weight is on the kids' shoulders. You need a hip belt—not just a thin nylon strap—for the backpack to be comfortable with a load for an extended period of time. Inappropriate backpacks can result in sore shoulders, aching hips, and a generally lousy attitude.

GO LIGHT

Today's backpacking trends focus on going light and fast. There are definitely tricks to pick up from this movement that will help you cut your weight and make hiking more comfortable, but with children be careful about cutting your corners too sharply. Miscalculations affect children more acutely than adults, who are better able to suffer some discomfort without jeopardizing their safety and enjoyment. So use caution.

That said, you can follow some of these light and fast backpacking principles in planning your trip:

» Consider gear that can be used for more than one purpose, such as using a water bottle for a cup and a pile jacket as a pillow.

» Take only what you need. You don't need to bring a 15-ounce tube of sunscreen for an overnight trip. Pare things down to relatively precise amounts. If you don't know what those amounts are, keep track and learn from experience. Small travel-size toiletries are great for backpacking trips.

» Share gear. If you are traveling with other families, compare equipment lists and get rid of redundancy. You don't all need to bring pots and pans or huge containers of bug repellent.

» Keep track of what you use. As you spend more time out with your children, you'll begin to realize that you can get by without some of the items deemed critical in the comfort of your home. It's worth taking notes and checking back after your trip to see where you can cut back. It may be you can bring less fuel or fewer diapers than you thought.

SANITATION

Diapers

For day hikes, just double-bag dirty diapers in plastic and carry them out. You may want to consider digging a cathole (a hole approximately 6 to 8 inches deep and 200 feet from water) for disposing feces. Scrape the solid material out of the diaper with a sturdy stick and bury both the stick and the feces in the cathole. You'll definitely want to do this if you are going to be out for an extended period of time. Your pack will be lighter if you aren't carrying several days worth of poopy diapers.

Plastic shopping bags come in handy for packing out dirty diapers.
MOLLY ABSOLON

For multiday trips you can scrape out diapers and lay them in the sun to dry. The solar radiation gets rid of some of the moisture in a soiled diaper, thereby helping lighten the load and reduce odor. But be careful not to leave these diapers unattended because they may attract animals.

I know people who bring cloth diapers with them on extended trips. They carry a collapsible bucket and will wash soiled diapers out at the end of the

day. The beauty of this system is that you have to carry fewer diapers (assuming it is sunny enough to dry the washed ones), but you have to be fairly motivated to do the laundry and you'll need to have plenty of water available. Make sure washing is done at least 200 feet from streams or lakes to prevent contamination. And take care to scrape out the diaper well before you begin washing. Use a mild, biodegradable soap and rinse thoroughly with hot water.

You can wash out dirty diapers in the backcountry with a little effort and some foresight. CHRIS NORTH

Urination

Don't worry too much about kids urinating in any special place when you are out camping or hiking. One of the beauties of being outdoors with children is that you don't have to run around looking for a bathroom if they have to go. In general have them avoid water (although near murky desert rivers, people often advocate peeing directly into the water—check with land managers first), and stay away from public areas such as your camp kitchen.

Catholes

For solid waste, bring a small plastic trowel to dig a cathole. A hole 6 to 8 inches deep should suffice. You'll want to help your child dig the hole to make sure it's done properly. Catholes need to be at least 200 feet from water and away from trails, campsites, and other gathering spots. I carry a little toilet kit for this purpose. It contains a trowel, a packet of wipes or roll of toilet paper, a garbage bag for soiled wipes and TP, and some hand sanitizer. Make sure you pack out any soiled wipes or toilet paper.

Hand washing

Fecal contamination is one of the leading causes of intestinal illness anywhere, but especially in the backcountry. It takes effort to practice good hygiene, especially with young children. Make sure you have them wash their hands frequently. Carry soap and set up a hand-washing station around camp. You can do this by hanging a water bag from a tree with a bottle of soap stashed nearby. With this kind of setup in place, it's easy for kids to wash their hands.

If you don't have soap handy, pour water over your children's hands and have them rub them vigorously to get clean. WILLY WARNER

EXTRAS

If your child is attached to a particular blanket or a stuffed animal, bring it with you. The familiarity and comfort these items provide far outweigh any possible negatives. This becomes especially true at night when you are trying to get your child to go to sleep in a strange place and a weird bed.

Bringing along a special toy helps kids feel at home in a strange place. MOLLY DORAN

Camping Equipment List by Ages

This age-specific list is designed for a three-day summer camping trip in temperate climates. For warmer, shorter trips, you'll need less; for longer, colder trips, take more.

CLOTHING

Kids get dirty and wet, so you'll need to bring a bit more clothing for them than you might bring for yourself.

Upper Layers

All Ages

1–2 base-layer tops such as synthetic, wool, or silk long-sleeved lightweight long underwear.

1–2 mid-layers such as pile or wool sweaters—Zip-up tops are more versatile than pullovers. Hoodies' built-in hat adds flexibility. If the weather doesn't warrant two sweaters, take a sweater and a vest for a bit more warmth.

1 rain jacket—Rain gear can serve as wind gear in most conditions. In the Rockies or Sierras, a lightweight breathable wind shirt is nice for breezy, cold days.

1–2 T-shirts

Parka (optional)—At high elevations summer temperatures can be cool at night, so you might want to consider bringing along an insulated parka with a hood.

(continued)

Babies

You can substitute a pair of polyester footie pajamas for one set of long underwear. These work great for sleeping and can serve as a good base layer on cold, rainy days. Footie pajamas with a hood are even better.

Lower Layers

All Ages

2 pairs base layers such as synthetic pants or long underwear—Nylon gym pants work great as do polypropylene long underwear.

1 pair rain pants

1 pair nylon shorts—Board shorts work well because they dry quickly.

2–3 pairs underwear (optional)—Some kids do fine going without underwear, especially on short trips, but it's definitely harder to stay clean. Try to find synthetic underwear if possible. Remember, wet cotton underwear will chill your child regardless of how many layers he is wearing.

Babies

Diapers—Keep track of the number of diapers you use on an average day at home. Pack two more than you anticipate using *per day* to ensure you have plenty. For example, for a three-day trip, pack six extra diapers.

Wipes, changing mat, diaper cream, plastic garbage bag, hand sanitizer.

Head
All Ages
1 warm hat
1 sun hat

Babies
Consider a balaclava to insulate your child's neck and ears as well as her head.

Hands
All Ages
Gloves or mittens (important even in the summer when it's rainy and cool).

Babies
Wool or synthetic socks or thumbless mittens work well for keeping babies' hands protected.

Feet
All Ages
2–3 pairs wool or synthetic socks
1 pair hiking shoes—Sneakers work fine for most kids.
1 pair water shoes (neoprene water shoes, mesh sneakers, etc.), rain boots, or galoshes

(continued)

Babies

Wool or synthetic tights can work well as socks for babies and toddlers (even boys) because they don't end up with a gap between the socks and pants, plus they stay on.

1 pair booties—The biggest trick with babies is keeping shoes on their feet. Here is where footie pajamas come in handy on cold days. Look for footwear that is roomy and comes up over the ankle for best coverage.

1 pair rain boots to keep feet dry

TOILETRIES

All Ages

1 toothbrush

1 travel-size tube toothpaste

1 travel-size package of wipes (good for kids of all ages)

1 small tube moisturizing cream—Kids' delicate skin, especially on hands and cheeks, gets easily chafed by wind and sun.

1 small tube sunscreen

Lip balm

Insect repellent

MISCELLANEOUS

All Ages

Sunglasses—Get the strap-on kind for babies and toddlers.

1 water bottle

Cup, bowl, and spoon

SLEEPING SYSTEM
All Ages
Sleeping bag—Avoid cheap, cotton-lined bags. Close-fitting mummy bags work best for warmth.
Sleeping pad

Babies and Toddlers
Most infants and toddlers can share a sleeping bag with a parent or sibling. Look for bag extenders to give you more room.

GEAR
Babies and Toddlers
1 baby backpack with sun and rain protection

Kids Ages 4–6
1 small hydration pack to carry water, a snack, and possibly a layer

Kids Ages 7–10
1 well-fitting backpack with hip belt—Backpacks without hip belts or with only a narrow nylon waist strap only work for very light loads.

Chapter Three
Food for Kids in the Outdoors

When I worked for the National Outdoor Leadership School, people used to talk about the need to HALT before you tackled a task or decision. HALT stood for hungry, angry, lonely, and tired and was a reminder to take care of these basic needs before you attempted anything that required attention, focus, or even basic civility. We just don't function very well when we are HALTing.

Children are more extreme than adults in their response to the components of HALT. Most parents have experienced times when everyone is melting down and it's utter chaos all because a magic snack or precious nap was missed. Children will let you know loudly and clearly when they are unhappy and need food and rest, even if they can't articulate exactly what is going on. For their benefit—and your own—it's imperative to have plenty of food on any hiking or camping trip.

Special treats like s'mores can be part of what kids look forward to on backpacking trips. SCOTT KANE

SNACKS

Choosing healthy snacks is great, but don't go too overboard. If you are active and outdoors all day, your kids deserve some special treats. My daughter will eat raisins and nuts when mixed with chocolate, so that's one way to sneak in something besides straight sugar. Fruit leathers are also good and have at least some nutrients. I often carry a stash of M&Ms or hard candies; treats that can be doled out slowly over tough sections of trail or at times when I really want my daughter to push on through rather than stop. I know people who've used candy to lure their children down the trail like the breadcrumbs in Hansel and Gretel. Finding the candy becomes a kind of treasure hunt and the kids end up moving along without even realizing it.

In addition to candy and sweets, bring sliced apples or pears, peelable fruit such as tangerines, even canned fruit packed in water for a nutritious and popular snack. Carrot sticks are another healthy alternative, as are celery with peanut butter and raisins. Basically you'll want variety and taste to encourage kids to eat along the way.

Baking quick breads using mixes like Bisquick allows kids to help with the cooking.
CAROLINE BYRD

BREAKFAST

Breakfast can be pretty straightforward. Kids usually like sweet hot cereals such as instant oatmeal or rice pudding with milk, cinnamon, and raisins. You can make chocolate chip pancakes for a special treat, creating faces with the chips to excite your child's appetite.

Homemade breads are also fun for breakfast. Kids love baking because the end product is usually tasty and because they can participate in the process. I remember as a child adoring a breakfast treat we called "doughboys." They were made from Bisquick and water mixed up into a tacky dough and then wrapped around a stick about the thickness of an adult thumb. We'd toast the dough over the fire and then eat it with honey or jelly.

You might want to consider investing in a lightweight aluminum reflector oven for backpacking. I remember using these ovens at summer camp for biscuits, coffee cake, and other yummy baked goods. A reflector oven is a shiny three-sided box with a shelf for a pan to rest on. You place the oven beside a blazing fire and the heat from the fire radiates off the shiny aluminum sides of the box, cooking your dough or batter. You can also bake on coals or by building a twiggy fire on top of a frying pan lid. See *Backpacker* magazine's *Campsite Cooking* for more detail on alternate cooking options.

Lunch on the trail begins after breakfast and ends with dinner and usually consists of a series of snacks rather than a single sit-down meal. WILLY WARNER

LUNCH

While you may end up snacking all day rather than sitting down for a full-blown lunch, you do want to bring along some food that has a bit more substance than the ones listed in the section on snacks for a midday meal. Lunch can be a peanut butter and jelly sandwich or my daughter's personal favorite: summer sausage and cheese. Your goal is to get some fats and protein into your kids to help them replace the calories they are burning during the course of the day. Cheese, tuna fish, salami, sausage, hard-boiled eggs, and nut butters such as peanut butter are all good sources of calories for hardworking children.

On cold, wet hikes kids need food like nuts with lots of fat, protein, and calories to keep them going.

PETER ABSOLON

DINNER

Making meals fun in the outdoors can add to your child's enjoyment of the entire experience. I remember clearly the "silver turtles" we used to eat on Girl Scout overnight trips back when I was a child. Our silver turtles were made from a hamburger patty, thinly sliced potatoes and carrots, and maybe a slice of cheese all wrapped up in aluminum foil and tossed into the coals of a campfire. Any combination of meat and vegetables will work. You'll need to have the ability to keep meat cool during the day, which may not be possible on a backpacking trip. But if you are being supported by animals or are just going out for one night in cool temperatures, you can indulge in this fun treat.

Make sure that you cook these foil meals on coals rather than a flaming fire, or you'll end up with food that is burned on the outside and raw in the middle. Build up the campfire before dinner until you have a good bed of hot coals, and then let the flames die down. Bury your meal packet in the coals and let sit for ten or fifteen minutes. You'll need to check the meat to make sure it is cooked through before eating.

Pita pizzas are another great kid meal. Just take pita bread, a can of tomato paste, and some cheese to make individual pizzas for everyone in your group. If you bring some extra toppings—olives, peppers, pepperoni—the kids can decorate their own pizzas, making faces or pictures with the goodies. Cook the pizzas in a covered frying pan over low heat. To help melt the cheese, add a few drops of water to the hot pan and cover quickly. The resulting steam will melt the cheese.

Catching and cooking fish—whether you fry them, grill them, or make fish chowder with little ones—is

also fun for kids. They feel a sense of accomplishment if they catch their own meal, though some children may balk at killing the fish.

Little fish can be used to make chowder, so everyone's catch can be eaten. SCOTT KANE

On trips with animal support, you may have access to coolers to keep food fresh. With this scenario you can make foods like spaghetti sauce or a stir-fry at home and freeze them in two-ply plastic bags. These frozen packs can then serve as "ice" in your cooler, gradually thawing out for a quick yummy dinner during the course of your trip.

It's also nice to bring along dried soup packages, ramen noodles, or instant potato flakes—foods that cook up quickly for immediate gratification after a long day or in cold, wet conditions.

Be creative to make even one-pot glop meals special; here a shell subs in for a bowl. SCOTT KANE

Finally, some basic comfort foods—such as good old mac and cheese—transfer well from home to the outdoors.

DESSERT

No all-American, kid-centered camping trip is complete without s'mores. You know: roasted marshmallows, chocolate, and graham crackers. Don't forget. Your child won't forgive you if you do.

You can also bring instant cheesecake mix or bake a cake in a reflector oven.

No kid-centered camping trip is complete without roasting marshmallows on a fire.
SCOTT KANE

DRINKS

Hot chocolate is a mainstay, but you may also want to consider bringing some powdered fruit drinks such as lemonade or fruit punch to mix up and help keep children hydrated while hiking. Kids often enjoy sweet tea or warm, spiced milk (cinnamon, sugar, and vanilla for example) as alternatives to hot cocoa.

Chapter Four

Trail Entertainment

As we all know, children have short attention spans and limited abilities to entertain themselves. This is especially true when they are doing something they perceive to be tedious or hard, such as going for a long car ride and, yes, sometimes a hike. The success of your trip will often be determined by how creative you can be at keeping your child entertained on the trail. Everyone has a trick or two, but you'll soon find out that you go through your repertoire quickly, so having a few more to draw on is very useful, especially on long, boring stretches of trail.

Be prepared to keep kids occupied on the trail. MOLLY ABSOLON

STORYTELLING

This is probably one of the most common diversion techniques I came across in my research for this book. It is certainly the one my family falls back on time after time. My daughter will walk for hours if we keep up the storytelling. We use a variety of tactics: We tell her stories, she tells us stories, and we make up stories together. We have a few characters who appear in different stories again and again, which helps for times when your creativity wanes. Finally, I confess that on one long trip we brought along an MP3 player loaded up with stories we'd gotten off the Internet. We were reluctant to rely too heavily on the player because we felt it took away from the natural world we were trying to explore, but it kept our daughter entertained for the final mile or so we needed to reach our destination after my husband and I both ran out of story ideas. I also have a friend who has read books to her kids while walking along flat sections of trail.

FAIRIES, IMAGINARY CREATURES, AND SUPERHEROES

My daughter loves to dream up different kinds of fairies as we hike. We'll go into great detail about how they look, what they are wearing, what powers they may have, and what their homes look like. We've made up moss fairies, water fairies, flower fairies, rain fairies; the list is endless really. I know other people who make up superheroes and magical creatures. The principles are the same: what do they look like, what can they do, and where do they live? Sometimes these creations can morph into stories, but usually we just set things up, taking turns making up different identities. What makes this game so effective is the back and forth dialog between adult and child. Together you dig into your imagination, drawing from things you see to come up with extraordinarily wonderful ideas and images.

The landscape can inspire all sorts of creative imaginings from your kids, such as flower fairies or superheroes. SCOTT KANE

I SPY AND TWENTY QUESTIONS

Playing "I Spy" can be tricky if you hike past the spied item before the guesser finishes, but it's a great way to get kids looking around. Just remember to find things that are not necessarily site-specific, so instead of the one dead tree you walk by, look for a type of tree that surrounds you. Try to be creative in the process. Challenge yourself and your kids to use their senses. Instead of saying "I spy a green shrub," say "I spy something that scratches my arms when I touch it and its fruit smells sweet" (raspberry bushes).

In "Twenty Questions" the guesser is allowed twenty yes/no questions and three guesses to figure out what item is being thought of. This game is less site-specific and, therefore, you don't have to work around the challenge of hiking past your object. Still, it's worth tying the game to your location and using it as a way for children to explore the area. Choose objects from the surrounding environment and use the game to call attention to the more subtle aspects of nature they may miss if they just walk down the trail with their heads down.

SCAVENGER HUNTS

Scavenger hunts are a great discovery tool for kids. You can come up with lists of varying difficulty for different age levels or have older children help younger ones find everything. Be creative. Make some items super easy: three different-shaped leaves or a colorful rock for example. Others can be hard or maybe even close to impossible: a feather, an animal track, or a bird's nest. Add in some human signs, such as litter or footprints. Have a prize—a snack, candy, or even a rest break can be good incentive for kids to finish their list. I tend to shy away from making my scavenger hunts competitive, but your kids may respond well to the challenge of finishing before their peers. I find that my daughter gets discouraged if she perceives that she is behind and loses interest in the hunt, but many children thrive on the element of competition, so you decide.

Scavenger hunts help kids notice animal tracks and other signs that they might miss otherwise. SCOTT KANE

TEACH A CLASS

Kids love to learn about the world around them. Find out some interesting trivia about the plants and animals you may see on your trip and talk to your kids about it on the trail. There are some wonderful natural history books out there that can help you identify plants and animals, learn about their medicinal, edible—even commercial—uses, and tell you about how things got their name. Discovering fun facts helps people—adults included—remember more and brings the landscape alive in a special way.

Taking time to learn something about your destination and sharing it with your children helps bring the landscape and its history alive. SCOTT KANE

Tell your kids how the landscape was formed, who used to live there, and what animals inhabit the area. You can talk about microclimates and compare the difference between a sunny dry slope and a moist shaded one. You can use props: Bend a Snickers bar to show how glaciers crack as they go around corners, and then eat up the visual aid. Chocolate can also be used to mimic animal signs, such as scat. Many people like to trick their kids into thinking they are eating scat by putting chocolate "poop" out on the ground to pop into their mouths. The point of the trick is to get the kids thinking about the animals that live in the area, but be sure to let them know you aren't eating real scat or you may have some unintended consequences. Edible plants are also fun for kids to try, but make sure you know what you are eating before you feed your child. Finally, in many parts of the United States—particularly the Colorado Plateau—you can find artifacts and ruins from past civilizations to explore in the backcountry. The mystery of these sites can captivate everyone's imaginations, even your own.

You may want to give your child a pair of small binoculars to carry so he can check things out on the trail. A hand lens can also be fun to bring along. Kids, and adults, are often amazed when they examine a dragonfly or a flower under magnification. You don't really need to know a lot of information to get kids thinking about the remarkable natural world you are exploring. It just takes modeling interest and a few fun tidbits of information to get kids looking, questioning, and coming up with their own theories for why things are the way they are.

Tools such as binoculars or a hand lens can help broaden a child's perspective.
MOLLY DORAN

CAMERAS

Give your child her own camera or perhaps one of those little video recorders to carry. Children love to document their journey through pictures and film and you may find they will keep themselves entertained for hours.

TRUST WALKS

On flat sections of trail, try blindfolding your child and leading him down the trail. Ask him what he perceives that he had missed before. You may need to prompt him by asking if he hears sounds or notices smells to help him clue into using his other senses. Give him opportunities to touch things along the way and to guess what they are. If you are stopped for a rest break, you can try to have him locate some of the objects he's touched after you remove the blindfold. For example, have him hug a tree and then walk away. Remove the blindfold and see if he can guess which tree he touched.

SING SONGS

Singing is a great way to pass the time on the trail. It helps to know more than a few words to a song, however. I went to summer camp for years and have a huge repertoire of songs to belt out along the trail. If you don't have your own repository of songs to draw from, you can buy a songbook. *Campfire Songs* by Irene Maddox and Rosalyn Cobb and *100 Songs for Kids: Sing-Along Favorites* by Dan Coates have lots of the old classics as well as some new ones you may not be familiar with.

MINUTE MYSTERIES, RIDDLES, PUZZLES, AND JOKES

If you know them, use them. You can find hundreds of minute mysteries and kids' riddles online for free; just Google "minute mystery" or "kids' jokes." Print out a page of ideas and you'll have something to ponder with your children when your other sources of inspiration begin to dry up. A paperback Mad Libs book can also provide entertainment as you hike. At a child's pace, you can usually manage to write in words and walk at the same time.

You may not find your children's sense of humor all that funny. It helps for kids to have friends or siblings along to share stories that amuse them but not you.
SCOTT KANE

NATURE JOURNALS

Nature journals don't do much for trail entertainment, but if you set it up so the kids are thinking about recording some of the things they've seen and done during the day, it can help keep them alert. Bring a small spiral notebook and pencils (colored ones if you want to be extravagant). Let the kids pull them out during rest breaks to draw a plant or lizard or to write down something they saw or learned during the course of the day.

Journals are a wonderful way to explore and record the world around you. SCOTT KANE

PROPS

You can bring along props for entertainment as well. I have friends who advocate carrying a lightweight kite to whip out on open ridgetops to keep their children engaged in the moment. Other props may be a Frisbee or a foam ball to toss around.

Peer Pressure

My daughter is an only child, so we've spent lots of time in the backcountry alone together. We have had great adventures out there, but it can be hard work at times. Traveling with other families makes everything easier. The kids keep each other entertained and motivated on the trail, and provide playmates for around camp so you can sit back and relax. Kids also compete, which can be an incentive to try harder. If Avery sees her friends walking down the trail without complaint, she'll do the same. Find like-minded families to travel with or bring along a buddy for your child to help make the camping or hiking experience more kid-centric.

PLAYING

Hiking doesn't have to be about pounding out the miles. I remember asking a friend about where to hike at Castle Hill in New Zealand. He said, "Head up the left path, drop your packs, take off your shoes, and start running—but don't forget where you leave your stuff." His advice was as philosophical as it was practical. Castle Hill, like many other magical outdoor destinations around the world, does not lend itself to a focused hike—especially with children. They are places to ramble, play, and explore. Places where you can spend hours and cover very little ground, but have an incredible experience in the natural world with your kids. So don't limit your definition of hiking to moving from point A to point B down a trail. Find places that allow you to wander and explore freely.

Don't let your goals blind you to the opportunities for play along the way. MOLLY DORAN

Dealing with Whining

You've told stories for hours, sung songs over and over again, organized scavenger hunts, and told every joke you have ever heard, and your child is still moping along, whining about how tired she is. We've all been there. We're tired, our shoulders and feet hurt, it's hot, and we still have miles to go before we can drop our pack and rest. The difference is, we know how to control ourselves and keep our misery inside. Kids don't have those filters. If they are uncomfortable, they will tell you. If you are sure the problem is not injurious and there is no easy remedy, you may just have to let them whine. Candy helps, but ultimately there may be those moments when the kid just has to keep walking. That's okay. Just try not to let it happen too often or she will learn to hate hiking.

CAMP ENTERTAINMENT

Your job as cruise director doesn't end once you pull into camp. Kids often still need something to do even when you are done hiking for the day. You can put them to work helping with the chores or cooking; take them fishing; or bring along a few toys for them to play with—especially if they have something they are particularly attached to.

Kids can get bored quickly, especially if they are used to lots of external stimulation and structured activities. Have things for them to do (such as going fishing) or to play with (such as a favorite toy or game) to keep them happy in camp. SCOTT KANE

Chapter Five

Supported Trips

In many parts of the country, you can hire animals to help you carry your load into the wilderness. With children, this assistance can allow you to go deeper into the mountains, farther down the trail, and for a longer duration on your trips, so it's worth considering.

HUMANS

Before I go into detail about animals, I should mention you can use humans to help you carry your load. Our first family backpacking trip took place when our daughter was less than two. We went with a child-less couple who were excited to go camping with a baby (not all people are). This arrangement meant we had three adults to carry the bulk of our gear and food, while the fourth carried our daughter. The plus side of this kind of setup is that it is free and you don't have to worry about dealing with animals. The key is to make sure your companions understand what it means to go camping with children: The kids are the center of your universe. You can't leave them alone, and you can't force them to push themselves. Your colleagues need to understand and accept these limitations to ensure your trip is a success.

Porters

In many parts of the world, you can hire porters to carry your loads from camp to camp. For example, Peru, Nepal, and India have well-established networks of professional porters available for hire. In the United States it's a bit trickier because we don't have the same kind of systems in place; however, you may be able to find someone who is willing to carry a load for you for a small fee. Try putting up a notice at an outdoor store or checking in with a college outing club to see if there are any willing people available. Protect yourself from potential scammers by asking for and checking references.

LLAMAS

A quick search for llama packing on the Internet reveals numerous outfitters located across the United States. Some offer guided pack trips; others rent llamas out for personal use. So if you are considering a backcountry overnight trip and are interested in using llamas for support, get online and look to see if you can find outfitters in the area.

I went on a llama-packing trip with a group of families a few summers ago. We had eleven adults, seven children, and seven llamas. My daughter was the oldest at seven and we had two babies in diapers. All of us had been professional outdoor leaders prior to having families, so it was quite a new adventure

Most llamas are docile and tolerant of children playing around them. SCOTT KANE

to be out with this huge gang of children and llamas. But the trip was wonderful and the llamas added a unique dimension to the experience, especially for the kids, who viewed them almost as pets.

Llama Pros

» Llamas are kid friendly. On our trip even the little ones were able to lead their llamas down the trail. The llamas were unfazed by children running around them or trying to feed them grass. They don't have tons of personality, seeming to prefer sitting chewing their cud with their noses in the air most of the time, but their indifference to us made them all the more reliable around the children.

» Llamas are low maintenance. They just need a bit of grass and some water to survive. We did not carry any supplemental feed although there may be places and times of the year when that is required. We were able to stake the llamas out in an open meadow and leave them for the day while we went off hiking. We moved their stakes occasionally and kicked around the piles of scat they left behind, but that was about the extent of the care they needed. You do have to be careful about overheating and it does require some training to ensure you know how to pack the animals properly, but overall llamas were relatively easy to work with.

» Llamas allow you to bring more gear. With two babies in diapers, we had a lot of stuff to carry. The llamas allowed us to hike with light packs and still bring along all the equipment we needed for our trip. How much weight they can carry depends on a number of variables such as terrain, conditioning, size, etc. They carry less than a horse or mule, but still more than I like to carry, about 70 to 80 pounds on average.

Llama Cons

» Llamas involve more logistics than just grabbing your pack and hitting the trail. Most outfitters require you to complete some kind of

Kids love leading llamas down the trail, even if the animals are not always cooperative. SCOTT KANE

training prior to taking off with their animals. You also have to plan ahead to guarantee the animals are available.

» Llamas are not free. The cost of renting llamas varies, but it's more than it costs to go without.

» Llamas are somewhat limited in where they can travel. Llamas do well on trails, especially flat, wide, smooth ones. Once the terrain gets steeper and rockier, they require some coercion and may refuse to negotiate some obstacles. Take time to talk to your outfitter about what routes are appropriate for llamas before getting excited about a rocky traverse only to have your llama refuse to follow. (Which they will. Llamas are known to sit down and refuse to budge if they are tired, uncomfortable, or sick of walking.)

HORSES AND MULES

Horses and mules are the traditional pack animal of choice in many parts of the country for good reason: They can carry very heavy loads and, furthermore, you can ride them if necessary or desired.

Horse and Mule Pros

» Horses and mules can carry big loads, probably twice the amount a llama can carry, which means you'll require fewer animals to support your trip. And, if you want, you can bring coolers, Dutch ovens, big wall tents—all the comforts of home—with horses and mules.

There's something quintessentially Western about horsepacking. The presence of horses adds a whole different aura to your outdoor experience. ALLEN'S DIAMOND 4 RANCH

Having horses for the kids to ride allows you to cover a lot more miles than if you just depended on their little legs. GARY WILMOT

» Outfitters are often willing to do drops and pickups for you. I once hired a horse packer to drop off and pick up equipment for a trip with my extended family—which included children and grandparents—allowing us to hike with light day packs and still have steaks and wine for dinner and a rack and rope for climbing.

» Packhorses can be led through the mountains if you do not want to ride (or don't have the skills to ride).

» Horses and mules are common in the West, so it's easy to locate outfitters to support your trip.

Horse and Mule Cons

» Horses and mules generally require more skill to use. You may be able to find a gentle old nag to lead around the mountains, but most likely you will need to hire a professional outfitter or guide to deal with the horses.

» Horses and mules are less kid friendly. You aren't going to be able to leave your children alone around most horses. Even the nicest animals are still big, prone to sudden fright, and somewhat unpredictable. You'll need to be vigilant and your kids will have less independence than they would around llamas or goats (see section on goat packing).

» Horses and mules generally require supplemental feed and lots of care around camp. It's work to pack horses and mules. That doesn't mean the work is without rewards; you just need to be prepared to care for the animals.

» Like all pack animals, horses and mules are not free. Depending on how you intend to use them, your cost will vary. Our drop-off/pickup was quite reasonable, but a fully supported horsepacking trip can be pricey.

GOATS

Agile, friendly, and easy to care for, goats are another pack animal that can help lighten your load. Most pack goats are wethers—or neutered males—so they don't have the rank smell associated with bucks. The aggressive reputation goats have in fairy tales (e.g., The Billy

Goat Gruff) is usually indicative of improper training rather than a bad temperament. The best pack goats are imprinted to humans from birth. As a result they are affectionate and won't wander far away from you on the trail or around camp. And they are great around kids because of their small size and gentle disposition.

Goat Pros

» Goats are light on the land. They forage like deer, browsing as they walk, and leave little impact on trails or around camp.

» Goats require little water (in areas with good forage they can go a day or two without drinking) and, depending on your destination, may not need supplemental food.

» Properly trained goats will follow you down the trail without a lead line and will sleep next to your shelter without being tied.

» Goats are easy to pack and you don't have to lift huge loads up high; most people, including bigger kids, can handle the effort.

» Goats are agile and capable of traveling over almost any terrain you can tackle (especially with children). This allows you to get a bit farther off the beaten path and avoid congested areas.

» Goats can be transported to and from the backcountry in the back of a pickup truck or in a small trailer.

Goats consider humans to be part of their herd and will follow closely without a lead. CHARLIE WILSON

Goat Cons

» Pack goats are less common than llamas or horses, so you may have a hard time finding animals to rent. Often pack goat outfitters require you to participate on a guided trip, which may not fit your budget or time frame. Of course, you may want to get your own goats—they are reported to be relatively easy keepers—but we won't go into that in this book.

» Goats are curious; they like to meander down the trail and you can't really rush them. That means they typically do not cover as much distance in a single day as other pack animals. That is probably just fine if you are traveling with children, however.

» Goats can carry diseases that are deadly for native bighorn sheep. If you are traveling to a destination that has bighorn sheep, check in with wildlife managers to make sure there are no special regulations for domestic goats to protect native bighorn populations.

Chapter Six

Yurts, Huts, and Forest Service Cabins

In many parts of the world, you can stay in huts, shelters, cabins, or yurts during overnight backcountry trips, saving you the hassle of carrying tents, sleeping pads, and sometimes even cooking paraphernalia. These facilities come in all shapes and sizes: In the Alps they may include restaurants and bars, while many of the shelters found along the Appalachian Trail are little more than three-sided lean-tos.

WHAT'S OUT THERE?

You'll need to do some research before you head out for a hut trip. Wilderness areas in the United States by definition do not contain any manmade structures (except in a few cases where the buildings were in place before the 1964 Wilderness Act was enacted); so if you are headed into wilderness with a capital W, don't expect to find permanent shelters along the trail. But there are parts of the country where huts are strategically located along popular trails, allowing travelers to go from one place to another without having to worry about providing their own sleeping quarters.

The Appalachian Mountain Club in New England and the 10th Mountain Division Hut Association in Colorado are among the United States' most established hut systems, but there are other options in many parts of the country. Worldwide, huts are popular in mountainous regions in Europe, Canada, New Zealand, and Japan, while many of the popular trekking routes in the Himalaya move from teahouse to teahouse. Sleeping arrangements range from simple dormitory rooms to private or semi-private rooms. Some huts include cooking facilities complete with stoves, utensils, and pots and pans so you can forego carrying any camping gear. You may even be able to purchase prepared meals or buy a few staples to cook with. The water and toilet provisions will also vary, ranging from simple pit toilets to running water and flush units. The cost of such accommodations reflects the refinement of the facilities: Deluxe rooms and hot showers will set you back a lot more than a simple dorm room with an outhouse.

There's lots of information on backcountry huts on the Internet, so just start searching. If you are traveling overseas, check with the country's land management agency to find out what kind of lodging options are available. For example, in New Zealand the website of the Department of Conservation (DOC) is the place to start planning your backcountry trip. Many countries have mountaineering associations that maintain alpine lodging facilities. Guidebooks can also give you an idea of the types of options available.

Huts can be great with children: They provide an enclosed facility where little ones have some freedom to roam without constant supervision; they allow you

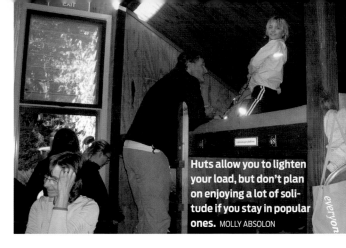

Huts allow you to lighten your load, but don't plan on enjoying a lot of solitude if you stay in popular ones. MOLLY ABSOLON

to escape the elements in the event of bad weather; and they usually have woodstoves to dry clothes and provide heat and comfort after a long day outdoors. Having a place to sleep indoors can be a nice way to ease your child into the idea of camping, especially if he or she is a bit intimidated by the idea of sleeping in a tent or having to go to the bathroom in the woods.

The flip side of huts is that you won't really be camping with your children. Huts are generally full of people and very social—the opposite of a lone tent tucked off the beaten track somewhere. If you are looking for solitude, huts probably won't be your thing.

Tips for Enhancing Your Hut Stay

» Bring earplugs. Your children probably won't notice the noise, but I know I'm a light sleeper and a dorm room full of strangers snoring or tossing and turning in their bags makes it hard for me to sleep. Earplugs help.

Yurts, Huts, and Forest Service Cabins

Huts are often located in spectacular settings. MOLLY ABSOLON

» Bring a light pair of slippers or booties. Some huts require you to remove your boots at the door. It's nice to have slippers to wear around inside and for quick trips outside to the toilet.

» Bring cards or games. Unlike tent camping where you tend to hit your sleeping bag fairly quickly after dinner, evenings are often quite social at most huts. You and your children will probably not be able to go to sleep too much before the rest of the guests, so it's nice to have some form of entertainment for after dinner. Games and cards are also a good way to integrate with others and get to know different people.

FOREST SERVICE CABINS

In many parts of the West and Alaska, the USDA Forest Service has cabins available for rent. These cabins sleep anywhere from four up to eight or ten, and most can be reserved in advance. Prices vary according to popularity and time of year but can range from $25 or so up to $45 per night. Check individual national forest websites for information on cabins near you. The cabins are often located fairly close to roads, serving as a great base for day hikes and an easy way to get your kids outdoors for a long weekend.

Other Options

You can find a wide variety of options for sleeping that don't involve carrying a tent, for instance eco-tourism camps with wall tents or campgrounds with cabins to rent. If you are interested in exploring these alternatives, get online and do some research.

Wall tents like these in India are just one camping option for ecotourists. MOLLY ABSOLON

Chapter Seven

Keeping Kids Safe in the Backcountry

Children have flourished in the wild forever. They can get wet and they aren't damaged by a little bit of dirt. You probably face more hazards taking them to the mall than you do going for a hike or camping trip. But we have a perception that it's dangerous out there in the land of lions and tigers and bears, so often we're afraid to go.

There are some real hazards in the outdoors—just as there are on the playground—and there are also lots of imaginary ones. The best strategy for traveling in the wild safely with children is to understand the risks and to develop strategies to limit your exposure.

RISK MANAGEMENT

Some professional outdoors people use the following equation to help them evaluate risk:

Risk = Likelihood x Consequences

The idea with this equation is that you look at a potential risk—say the risk of falling while crossing a creek—and determine first how likely it is you or your child will fall, and then what happens if you do. Wading across a mellow stream is unlikely to cause you to fall and even if you do, you'll just get wet, so the risk is low. On the other hand it's highly likely you may fall off a slippery log. If you land in a pool of water, you'll just get wet, so again the risk is low. But if you fall into a raging torrent of whitewater, the consequences of a fall are high. You could be injured or killed; therefore it is probably not worth the risk to attempt such a crossing.

The risk equation is a useful tool for evaluating decisions dispassionately and may help you avoid dangerous situations for yourself and your kids. It's also a good way to frame your decision making in discussions with your children. Talk through your thought process out loud with kids when evaluating hazards. Role modeling thoughtful risk management is an important way to begin establishing good decision-making habits in your children.

OBJECTIVE HAZARDS

Objective hazards are real, physical threats to our well-being. To determine what these are, ask yourself what in the surrounding environment can kill or maim you—or more importantly, kill or maim your children? In the outdoors the answer to that question includes things like moving water, rockfall, weather, and in rare cases, dangerous animals. Awareness of these risks is the first step in avoiding them. Be conscious of your surroundings. Consider whether your position exposes you to any particular hazards. Is there a large river nearby? A glacier or boulder field? Are you in grizzly bear country? If the answer to any of these questions is yes, do you need to take precautions to protect yourself and your children?

Assess conditions carefully before venturing out onto snow with children. SCOTT KANE

When water gets above your knees it can push you around and be difficult to cross; don't forget that what is midshin for you will be thigh deep for your child. MOLLY DORAN

The Kid Factor

You don't have to avoid camping by a stream simply because your child could fall into the water and drown, but you do want to be aware of that possibility and take precautions. With young children your primary strategy for avoiding objective hazards will be supervision. Small children need monitoring so they don't wander away from camp and get into trouble. You may want to have one person specifically assigned to keep tabs on the kids at all times. The kids can help around camp or play—whatever you deem appropriate—but the adult in charge of the children should have no other distracting duties to keep them from their task.

Kids do not have a well-developed sense of danger; supervise them carefully to prevent problems. Heights, nearby water, and fires and stoves require the constant attention of at least one adult. SUZANNE LILYGREN

As children get older, they can take a more active role in their safety. Talk to kids about the potential risks along the trail or around camp, and discuss with them ways to mitigate hazards. Education is a powerful tool for getting children to understand the dangers without resorting to threats. Set boundaries around camp and define any unacceptable behaviors. Have everyone carry whistles and identify a code for communicating. For example: One loud blast can mean "come back to camp," two may mean "help," three "okay," etc.

If you feel as if your children aren't getting it, a simple demonstration can help. You can throw a stick into a river and watch the way it gets tossed around and pulled downstream to illustrate the power of moving water. Or maybe you want to wade out into the current with your child to let her feel the shock of the cold temperature and the pull of the current against her body.

You may require some equipment to manage risks appropriately. For example, most problems with bears occur after the animals are drawn into campsites by the smell of food. To avoid accidentally attracting bears and risking a dangerous encounter, you need to be able to store your food in some kind of bear-proof container such as a specially made plastic bear tube. Weather is another risk factor that can usually be mitigated effectively with proper equipment. Make sure your child has waterproof rain gear and appropriate footwear to keep her warm and dry regardless of conditions. If your child is riding on your back, invest in a beefy rain cover for your

If your campsite is beside a lake and your kids don't know how to swim, have them wear PFDs when playing on the shoreline to limit your stress and protect them from drowning. WILLY WARNER

child carrier to keep out the elements. Other potentially lifesaving gear may include a personal flotation device (PFD) or perhaps a rope.

SUBJECTIVE HAZARDS

Subjective hazards are the ones in our heads. For example: that feeling of paralyzing fear that overcomes you when you can't do a climbing move even though you are on a toprope and the worst that can happen if you fall is you'll end up hanging from the rope. Logic has little to do with our emotions in these kinds of situations, but it helps to understand that some dangers are made up in our brains. Kids have very little self-awareness and are often not able to assess their skills accurately. Some children will try anything, others are timid and reluctant.

You can help your child by acting as a filter and choosing appropriate challenges for his abilities. Talking about degrees of risk may help him learn to differentiate between something that is truly dangerous, such as an unprotected fall off a cliff, and something that just looks kind of scary, like hanging from the rope on a climb.

Don't belittle your child's fear; help him work through it so he understands what the real dangers are and what he has manufactured in his mind. The ability to separate objective from subjective hazards is an invaluable life skill.

FIRST AID

Regardless of all our precautions, there are times someone gets hurt. Most likely for children in the outdoors, it will be a small scrape or a case of poison ivy, but you may run into more serious injuries or illnesses. For most of us the worst thing in such a situation is the inability to help. If you plan to go hiking and backpacking with your children, take a first-aid course. It's unlikely you'll ever need advanced skills, but if your child is injured and you have no idea what to do, you'll be sorry you did not seek training.

This book is not a first-aid book, so I won't go into details about responding to emergencies (see *Backpacker* magazine's *Trailside First Aid* in the Core Skills series for more information). There are, however, a few considerations specific to children that are worth mentioning.

» **Ouchies:** The most common problem you are likely to experience in the backcountry with kids is small scrapes and cuts. Make sure to stock your first-aid kit with lots of Band-Aids. Just as at home, a Band-Aid goes a long way in helping ease the pain of a cut for kids. But take care to clean the wound well before covering it up. Skin infections are more common in the backcountry because you don't bathe regularly, so you need to take some extra precautions to prevent further problems.

» **Heat and Cold:** As mentioned earlier, children's thermal regulatory systems are not as well developed as an adult's. They aren't as good at staying cool when it's hot, and their small size and relatively large surface area means they lose heat quickly when it's cold. They also tend to ignore thermal discomfort longer than we do, so by the time it becomes apparent that they are cold, they are really cold. Watch your children and help them stay ahead of the game in maintaining a comfortable body temperature. If you feel cold, chances are your children feel cold so check in and help them layer up to get warm.

> Give kids a chance to acclimate. If you are hiking in the summer, ease into the rigors of your trip so they have time to get used to exercising in the heat. Take breaks in the middle of the day to avoid the hottest temperatures. Seek shade and encourage children to drink lots of water and eat food to maintain their electrolyte balance. If your kids are reluctant to drink plain water, bring along powdered drink mixes for flavor. Just remember: Kids aren't great about self-care. You need to watch out for them.

> Watch out for too much sun exposure too. If you are up in the mountains, the sunlight is more intense and can cause burning quickly. Make sure your kids wear sunscreen, sun hats, and sunglasses to protect their eyes from the glare.

> **Illness:** It is scary when your kids get sick in town, scarier when you are out in the bush. Make sure your first-aid kit contains fever-reducing pain medication such as children's acetaminophen or ibuprofen, as well as anti-diarrheal treatments. Kids are particularly susceptible to dehydration, and any illness that prevents them from keeping in liquids can become dangerous over time.

Worldwide, one of the most frequent causes of death in children under the age of five is diarrhea, so if your child gets sick, monitor her carefully, try to keep her hydrated, and seek medical help quickly if you cannot.

» **Bugs:** Young children do not swat away mosquitoes and they often react quite strongly to bites, so make sure to cover them up. Science has shown that low concentrations of DEET-based insect repellents are safe. However, use common sense in your application. Remember that young kids are likely to put fingers in their mouths and rub their eyes, so it's best not to apply repellent to their hands.

    » If you are out in tick season, make sure to do full-body checks at night before bed. Ticks carry all sorts of diseases; it's important to remove them before they have time to bite. Look carefully in warm, dark places: The groin area, armpits, and along the hairline are favorite spots for ticks to dig in. I remember finding two of these nasty critters tucked inside my daughter's ear one evening after a day spent out in the sagebrush. Now I check religiously over all of our bodies.

» **Rashes:** Watch out for poison ivy, poison oak, or other irritating plants and help your children learn to identify them to avoid an uncomfortable encounter. If you suspect your child has gotten into poison ivy or oak, try to wash off her skin as quickly as possible to minimize the irritation. Include an anti-itch cream such as hydrocortisone or calamine lotion in your first-aid kit to help ease the itching. Stinging nettles can also cause severe discomfort for children. Fortunately, that pain usually passes quickly. Your main treatment will probably be comforting your child while the sting endures. If you have aloe vera gel in your first-aid kit, apply it to the affected area for some relief.

First-Aid Kits

If you plan to spend a fair bit of time in the backcountry, it's worth investing in a first-aid kit. You can buy premade kits from outdoor equipment companies for a reasonable price and they usually come in a compact, convenient case for ease of access and portability. When traveling with children, it's usually worth adding a few child-specific items, such as children's Tylenol or ibuprofen, Benadryl, anti-itch cream, diaper cream, teething ointment, and lots of colorful Band-Aids.

Chapter Eight

Leave No Trace

Our wild lands are popular. Many of the most visited outdoor destinations attract thousands of people a year. The Leave No Trace Center for Outdoor Ethics has come up with a set of seven principles designed to help minimize the impact of people on the land. The goal of these principles is to allow us to love natural places without destroying them from overuse. Children often get excited about the idea of leaving no trace. For them the idea of hiding the signs of their passing can be a kind of game, and you may find them telling you when you have violated the rules.

SEVEN PRINCIPLES OF LEAVE NO TRACE

Plan Ahead and Prepare

- » Know the regulations and special concerns for the area you'll visit.
- » Prepare for extreme weather, hazards, and emergencies.
- » Schedule your trip to avoid times of high use.
- » Visit in small groups when possible. Consider splitting larger groups into smaller groups.
- » Repackage food to minimize waste.

Travel and Camp on Durable Surfaces

» Durable surfaces include established trails and campsites, rock, gravel, dry grasses, or snow.

» Protect riparian areas by camping at least 200 feet from lakes and streams.

» Good campsites are found, not made. Altering a site is not necessary.

» **In popular areas:** Concentrate use on existing trails and campsites.

  » Walk single file in the middle of the trail, even when wet or muddy.

  » Keep campsites small. Focus activity in areas where vegetation is absent.

» **In pristine areas:** Disperse use to prevent the creation of campsites and trails.

  » Avoid places where signs of past visitors are just beginning.

Dispose of Waste Properly

» Pack it in, pack it out. Inspect your campsite and rest areas for trash or spilled foods. Pack out all trash, leftover food, and litter.

» Deposit solid human waste in catholes dug 6 to 8 inches deep at least 200 feet from water, campsites, and trails. Cover and disguise the cathole when finished.

» Pack out toilet paper and hygiene products.

» To wash yourself or your dishes, carry water 200 feet away from streams or lakes and use small amounts of biodegradable soap. Scatter strained dishwater.

Leave What You Find

» Preserve the past: Examine, but do not touch, cultural or historic structures and artifacts.
» Leave rocks, plants, and other natural objects as you find them.
» Avoid introducing or transporting nonnative species.
» Do not build structures or furniture or dig trenches.

Minimize Campfire Impacts

» Campfires can cause lasting impacts to the backcountry. Use a lightweight stove for cooking and enjoy a candle lantern for light.
» Where fires are permitted, use established fire rings, fire pans, or mound fires.
» Keep fires small. Only use sticks from the ground that can be broken by hand.
» Burn all wood and coals to ash, put out campfires completely, and then scatter cool ashes.

Respect Wildlife

» Observe wildlife from a distance. Do not follow or approach them.
» Never feed animals. Feeding wildlife damages

their health, alters natural behaviors, and exposes them to predators and other dangers.

» Protect wildlife and your food by storing rations and trash securely.
» Control pets at all times, or leave them at home.
» Avoid wildlife during sensitive times: mating, nesting, raising young, or winter.

Be Considerate of Other Visitors

» Respect other visitors and protect the quality of their experience.
» Be courteous. Yield to other users on the trail.
» Step to the downhill side of the trail when encountering pack stock.
» Take rest breaks and camp away from trails and other visitors.
» Let nature's sounds prevail. Avoid loud voices and noises.

Chapter Nine

A Final Word

Hiking and backpacking with children is an adventure, and like all adventures, there are definite ups and downs to the experience. Those moments when you are wet, tired, and hungry and you need to change a diaper in the driving rain are not fun, but they are usually balanced by the laughter you share with your kids when you reach the summit of a peak (regardless of its height) or while sitting around a campfire telling ghost stories.

Watching my daughter scramble over boulders with ease and grace fills my heart with pride. I never even saw a snowcapped mountain until I was a teenager—let alone walked through a boulder field—and here my daughter is comfortable, confident, and capable in challenging terrain and variable conditions. Unlike me at her age, Avery at ten is as at home in the mountains as she is in town after years spent hiking and backpacking.

Spending time with your kids outdoors creates a closeness that is often elusive in our busy lives back home. MOLLY ABSOLON

Remember to pick destinations that are fun for kids. Remember to be flexible with your goals and change plans when things go awry. Remember to let your children help plan your trips and choose your goals. And remember that the experience is really more about them than you.

Time slows down when you get outdoors with your kids. You have time to play together without worrying about what's next on your to-do list. MOLLY DORAN

As I write this, my daughter is not far from puberty—a milestone I approach with some trepidation based on my own experience at that challenging age. Even now, she is usually more interested in hanging out with her friends than she is with me. But that changes when we hit the trail or head out for a camping trip. Away from home and her pack of friends, our intimacy is restored. We have fun together. We laugh, we work hard, we share stories, we enjoy an experience that stays with us and keeps us close even as her life becomes more and more independent of mine. It's worth every bit of effort it takes to create these shared memories, that closeness between parent and child, and to bring simple joy into our complicated lives. So go on, get out there.

If you start when your child is young, you'll build a lifetime of memories together. PETER ABSOLON

INDEX

ABOUT THE AUTHOR

Molly Absolon is a former NOLS instructor, an environmental educator, and outdoor writer. She is the author of the *Backpacker* magazine's *Campsite Cooking, Trailside Navigation, Trailside Recipes, Trailside First Aid,* and *Outdoor Survival*. She has recently moved to Victor, Idaho.